Nita Mehta's
Mexican
cooking

Nita Mehta

B.Sc. (Home Science), M.Sc. (Food and Nutrition), Gold Medalist

SNAB

Nita Mehta's
Mexicain
Recipes

ISBN 81-7869-122-1

Exclusive Distributor:

AMPRODUCTIONS
DIVISION OF: INFORMATION SCIENCE INDUSTRIES (CANADA) LIMITED

1169 Parisien St., Ottawa, Ont., K1B 4W4,
Tel: 613.745.3098 Fax: 613.745.7533
e-mail: amproductions@rogers.com
web: www.amproductions.ca

Published by:

SNAB
Publishers Pvt. Ltd.
3A/3 Asaf Ali Road,
New Delhi - 110002
Tel: 23252948, 23250091
Telefax:91-11-23250091
INDIA

Editorial and Marketing office:
E-159, Greater Kailash-II, N.Delhi-48
*Fax:*91-11-29225218, 29229558
*Tel:*91-11-29214011, 29218727, 29218574
E-Mail: nitamehta@email.com, nitamehta@nitamehta.com
*Website:*http://www.nitamehta.com
Website: http://www.snabindia.com

Printed at:
BRIJBISA ART PRESS LIMITED

Price: $ 5.95

Contents

Introduction   4
International Conversion Guide   5
Basic Ways of Folding Tortillas   6
Basic Recipes of Mexican Cuisine   7

soups & salads   12

Cilantro Soup   13
Red Bean & Chickpea Salad in Mango Dressing   14

snacks   16

Nachos with Salsa   17
Chicken Tacos   18
Spinach Quesadillas   20
Chilli Rellenos (Stuffed Chillies)   22

main dishes   24

Red Snapper Veracruz-Style   25
Chicken Chilli Chimichangas   26
Tex Mex Beans with Dumplings   29
Chicken Burritos with Sauce   30
Fajitas   32
Shrimps/Prawns in Pumpkin Seed Sauce   34
Veggie Enchiladas   36
Mutton Mince & Bean Pie   38
Bean & Corn Burritos   40

rice   42

White Pilaf with Cheese   43
Spicy Shrimp Pilaf   44

desserts   46

Rice Pudding   47

Glossary of Names/Terms   48

Introduction

*M*exican food is full of colour and vigour. It is one of the oldest cuisines of the western world and adapts itself well to everyday cooking as well as to entertaining.

Every cuisine grows out of its natural environment, its climate and the crops that grow there – in this case corn, which flavours so much of Mexican food, especially tortillas. Tortillas are the base of most of their main dishes. They are folded, filled and cooked in a variety of ways, as I have explained in the following pages.

Most people are familiar with nachos and burritos. In this book you will discover the full range – fajitas, enchiladas, quesadillas, pies and pilafs. I have enjoyed testing and perfecting every recipe for you. Join me in this voyage of discovery of an ancient and exciting cuisine!

Nita Menta

INTERNATIONAL CONVERSION GUIDE

These are not exact equivalents; they've been rounded-off to make measuring easier.

WEIGHTS & MEASURES

METRIC	IMPERIAL
15 g	½ oz
30 g	1 oz
60 g	2 oz
90 g	3 oz
125 g	4 oz (¼ lb)
155 g	5 oz
185 g	6 oz
220 g	7 oz
250 g	8 oz (½ lb)
280 g	9 oz
315 g	10 oz
345 g	11 oz
375 g	12 oz (¾ lb)
410 g	13 oz
440 g	14 oz
470 g	15 oz
500 g	16 oz (1 lb)
750 g	24 oz (1½ lb)
1 kg	30 oz (2 lb)

LIQUID MEASURES

METRIC	IMPERIAL
30 ml	1 fluid oz
60 ml	2 fluid oz
100 ml	3 fluid oz
125 ml	4 fluid oz
150 ml	5 fluid oz (¼ pint/1 gill)
190 ml	6 fluid oz
250 ml	8 fluid oz
300 ml	10 fluid oz (½ pint)
500 ml	16 fluid oz
600 ml	20 fluid oz (1 pint)
1000 ml	1¾ pints

CUPS & SPOON MEASURES

METRIC	IMPERIAL
1 ml	¼ tsp
2 ml	½ tsp
5 ml	1 tsp
15 ml	1 tbsp
60 ml	¼ cup
125 ml	½ cup
250 ml	1 cup

HELPFUL MEASURES

METRIC	IMPERIAL
3 mm	1/8 in
6 mm	¼ in
1 cm	½ in
2 cm	¾ in
2.5 cm	1 in
5 cm	2 in
6 cm	2½ in
8 cm	3 in
10 cm	4 in
13 cm	5 in
15 cm	6 in
18 cm	7 in
20 cm	8 in
23 cm	9 in
25 cm	10 in
28 cm	11 in
30 cm	12 in (1ft)

HOW TO MEASURE

When using the graduated metric measuring cups, it is important to shake the dry ingredients loosely into the required cup. Do not tap the cup on the table, or pack the ingredients into the cup unless otherwise directed. Level top of cup with a knife. When using graduated metric measuring spoons, level top of spoon with a knife. When measuring liquids in the jug, place jug on a flat surface, check for accuracy at eye level.

OVEN TEMPERATURE

These oven temperatures are only a guide. Always check the manufacturer's manual.

	°C (Celsius)	°F (Fahrenheit)	Gas Mark
Very low	120	250	1
Low	150	300	2
Moderately low	160	325	3
Moderate	180	350	4
Moderately high	190	375	5
High	200	400	6
Very high	230	450	7

Basic Ways of Folding Tortillas

Many Mexican dishes are made with tortillas. The difference lies in filling, folding and cooking.

Burritos

Burritos are flour tortillas rolled with a filling inside them. They are either warmed or pan-fried and served as the main meal.

Chimichangas

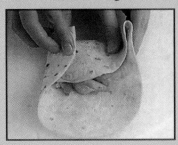

Chimichangas are tortillas that are filled then folded like envelopes. They are fried till crisp and served as the main meal.

Enchiladas

Enchiladas are tortillas in which the filling is laid down the center. The tortilla is then rolled to make a tube. The tubes are topped with cheese and baked. They are served as the main meal.

Flautas

Flautas are tortillas that are filled, rolled very tightly into a flute shape and fried. They are served as a snack.

Tostadas

Tostadas are small round flour tortillas that are fried to a crisp golden colour and then topped with different toppings. They are mainly served as a snack.

Tacos

Tacos are corn tortillas that have been folded and fried in hot oil. A filling is inserted into the crisp taco shells. They are served as a snack. Taco shells are also available ready-made.

Basic Recipes of Mexican Cuisine

All basic recipes can be made 1-2 days in advance, and reheated and used as required.

Tortillas

Tortillas are thin chappatis made of plain flour (maida), or whole wheat flour (atta) or corn meal (makki ka atta). The most common ones are the flour tortillas. Most of the Mexican dishes are made with tortillas. The difference lies in the filling, folding and cooking. They are used in many different ways for a Mexican meal. Tortillas can be prepared and kept well sealed in a plastic bag for 1-2 days in the fridge or even frozen for a few days. Just warm before using them so that they can be easily folded and used as required.

Flour Tortillas

Makes 7 Tortillas

INGREDIENTS

1½ cups flour (*maida*), ½ tsp salt
3 tbsp oil
¼ cup warm water to make the dough (approx.)

METHOD

1 Mix flour, salt and oil together.

2 Add warm water gradually and make a smooth and elastic dough.

3 Cover with a moist cloth (dipped in water and squeezed well) and keep aside for ½ an hour.

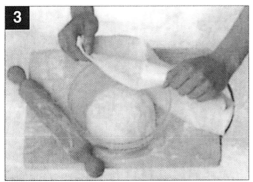

4 Divide the dough into 7 balls.

5 Roll out each part using a little dry flour if needed, into a large thin tortilla.

6 Heat a griddle. Place the rolled tortilla on the griddle. Cook lightly on one side for about a minute and then turn. Reduce heat and cook the other side also for 15-20 seconds till light brown specks appear. Remove from heat.

7 Keep warm tortillas wrapped in a cloth napkin or foil.

Note: *Do not overcook tortillas, otherwise they do not remain soft and will not roll well. Always wrap tortillas in a thick cloth napkin or in foil to keep them soft.*

Corn Tortillas

Makes 11-12 Tortillas

INGREDIENTS

1½ cups corn meal (*makai ka atta*)
1 cup flour (*maida*), ¾ tsp salt

METHOD

1 Mix corn meal, flour and salt in a big bowl. Knead with warm water to make a firm, yet pliable dough. Cover with a moist cloth and keep aside for 1 hour.

2 Divide dough into 11-12 balls. Roll into a large, flat, thin, round tortilla.

3 Heat a griddle. Place tortilla on the griddle. Cook for a minute on medium heat.

4 Turn over and cook the other side for a minute or till brown specks start appearing. Do not make them crisp. Remove from heat.

5 Make all the tortillas and keep them warm, wrapped in foil or cloth in a casserole. Use as required.

Sour Cream

Although sour cream is easily available, this homemade version is much lighter.

Serves 4

INGREDIENTS

1½ cups yogurt - hang for 1 hour in a
muslin cloth and squeeze lightly
¼ cup fresh cream, approx.
1 tsp lemon juice, or to taste
¼ tsp salt, or to taste

METHOD

1 Whisk hung yogurt till very smooth. Gradually add just enough cream to get a soft dropping consistency.

2 Add salt & lemon juice. Mix lightly. Keep in the refrigerator till serving time.

Roasted Tomato Salsa

Salsa simply means sauce. It is an essential and multipurpose accompaniment to all the Mexican dishes. It can be poured on the food, served as a relish, used as a dip with nacho chips or as a filling for tortillas, or as a dressing for salads.

Makes 1 cup

INGREDIENTS

5 tomatoes
1 tbsp oil
2 tbsp tomato ketchup
2 tbsp chopped cilantro/coriander
1 onion - chopped finely (½ cup)
2 green chillies - chopped
1 tsp vinegar, ½ tsp salt, ¼ tsp pepper
½ tsp sugar or to taste

METHOD

1   Roast all tomatoes under the grill till the skin turns blackish and charred. Cool and peel. Do not wash after peeling.

2   Chop 2 tomatoes and puree the other 3 tomatoes in a mixer.

3   Heat 1 tbsp oil, add chopped onion and green chillies. Cook till onion turns soft.

4   Add all the other ingredients and cook for 2 minutes. Do not cook further. Remove from heat.

Pineapple Salsa

Add ½ cup of very finely chopped ripe pineapple along with the other ingredients at step 4. Add seasonings to taste.

Refried Beans

Refried does not mean fried again as the name implies. It simply means beans that have been cooked thoroughly. Infact the beans are almost mashed to a paste. These beans are used in a lot of recipes as a filling and are very popular in Mexico.

Makes 1½ cups

INGREDIENTS

1 cup black beans or red kidney beans (*rajmah*)
½ onion - chopped (¼ cup)
2 flakes garlic - finely chopped
1 tomato - chopped
3 tbsp oil or butter
½ tsp red chilli powder, 1¼ tsp salt

METHOD

1 Clean and soak the beans in water overnight or at least for 6-8 hours.

2 Place beans in a pan with ½ of the chopped onion, garlic, tomato and 3 cups water. Cover and boil till beans turn tender. Let the water evaporate a little. Remove from heat.

3 Mash the boiled beans with the back of a ladle. Keep beans aside.

4 Heat oil/butter. Add the remaining chopped onion.

5 Fry till soft. Add beans along with the water.

6 Add salt and red chilli powder. Mix well. Bring to a boil. Lower heat and cook covered for 10 minutes, stirring and mashing occasionally. Serve hot or cold or as required.

Guacamole

Guacamole is a dip. People who may not appreciate avocado will love it in the form of this delicious dip, served with corn chips, or as a filling for tortillas, or even as a dressing for salads.

Makes 1½ cups

INGREDIENTS

1 blackish, ripe avocado
1 small onion - finely chopped
2 green chillies - finely chopped
1 tomato - deseeded and finely chopped
2 tsp finely chopped garlic
½ cup finely chopped cilantro/coriander
1¼ tsp salt, or to taste
3-4 tbsp lemon juice

METHOD

1 Cut an avocado in half. Remove the stone. Scoop out pulp from the avocado with a spoon.

2 Mash pulp with a fork. Add all other ingredients. Mash some more with the fork. Serve chilled or at room temperature.

Note: *Cover with a plastic wrap/cling film as guacamole tends to turn brown on keeping.*

Tip: *Always choose a ripe avocado as the unripe ones can be bitter. The ripe ones feel soft when pressed lightly and the green colour starts turning blackish. The seasonings will depend on the avocado as sometimes it is quiet bland and then you may want to add some more lemon juice or even a little more garlic paste or some olive oil to it.*

soups & salads

Cilantro Soup

Fresh coriander leaves, called cilantro, give their flavour to this fragrant soup.

Serves 3-4

INGREDIENTS

1 tsp butter
1 bay leaf (*tej patta*)
1" stick cinnamon (*dalchini*)
¾ cup chopped potato
1 cup cilantro/coriander - chopped with the stalks
½ cup milk
2½ cups ready-made stock/broth

METHOD

1. Peel potato and cut into small cubes or pieces.

2. Melt 1 tsp butter in a pan, add bay leaf, cinnamon and chopped potato. Cook for 5 minutes on medium heat, stirring occasionally.

3. Add 1 cup chopped cilantro coriander, cook for 1 minute.

4. Reduce heat. Add ½ cup milk. Cook for 2 minutes on medium heat, stirring continuously.

5. Remove from heat. Let it cool. Puree in a mixer.

6. Return puree to the pan, add the prepared stock. Give 2-3 boils. Remove from heat. Serve hot in individual soup bowls.

Red Bean & Chickpea Salad in Mango Dressing

Serves 8-10

INGREDIENTS

½ cup red kidney beans (*rajmah*)
½ cup chickpeas (*safeed/kabuli channas*)
1 cup grapes (black or green) or 1 cup peeled segments of orange
1 small green bell pepper - thinly sliced
1 onion - thinly sliced
2 tomatoes - seeded and thinly sliced

MANGO DRESSING

4 tbsp mango pulp
4 tbsp olive oil
½ tbsp honey
1 tbsp lemon juice, 1 tsp salt
¼ cup chopped cilantro/coriander leaves
1 tbsp crushed garlic
2 green chillies - chopped
1 tsp ground cumin (*jeera powder*)

METHOD

1 Soak kidney beans and chickpeas for 2 hours in hot water.

2 Put kidney beans, chickpeas, 1 cup water and ½ tsp salt in a pressure cooker. Pressure cook to give 1 whistle. Reduce heat and cook for 4-5 minutes. Do not cook longer. Remove from heat. Let the pressure drop by itself. Drain. The beans and chickpeas should turn soft but still be firm.

3 Place boiled kidney beans, chickpeas, grapes or orange, green bell pepper, onion and tomatoes in a bowl. Mix well.

4 Place all the ingredients of the dressing in a mixer and blend to a smooth puree.

5 Pour the dressing over the salad and mix well. Chill for 1 hour and serve chilled.

snacks

Nachos with Salsa

Nachos are fried tortilla chips. They go well with drinks. They can be made 5-6 days in advance & stored in an airtight container. They taste great with salsa.

Serves 4-5

INGREDIENTS

¾ cup maize flour/corn meal (*makai ka atta*)
½ cup plain flour (*maida*)
½ tbsp oil, ¾ tsp salt, ½ tsp oregano

TO SERVE
tomato salsa, (see p. 9)

METHOD

1 Sift both flours and salt together. Add oil and oregano. Mix well.

2 Knead to a stiff dough of rolling consistency, with about ¼ cup warm water. Knead well till smooth and cover and keep aside for 30 minutes. After 30 minutes, knead the dough again.

3 Make small marble sized balls. Roll out into thin tortillas, as thin as you can on a floured board. If the edges break while rolling, do not bother. Roll out thinly into a big round, like a chappati. Prick the round with a fork all over so that they do not puff on frying.

4 Cut the round into 4 pieces to get 4 triangles. Cut each triangle further into 2 pieces to get 8 triangular pieces. Make triangles in this way with the remaining dough.

5 Deep-fry 8-10 minutes on medium heat till they turn light golden. Do not make them dark in colour. Remove from oil on paper napkins.

6 Fry all triangles. Transfer to a clean dry pan. Sprinkle 1 tbsp flour on them. Gently toss to coat flour on the nachos to absorb any excess oil. Serve with salsa.

Chicken Tacos

These taco shells have a spicy chicken filling topped with salad and salsa. Serve them as a hearty snack.

Serves 6

INGREDIENTS

6 ready-made taco shells

CHICKEN FILLING
2 tbsp oil
250 g/8 oz chicken with bones
1 large onion - finely chopped (1 cup)
1½ tsp chopped garlic
2 large tomatoes - finely chopped (1 cup)
1 green chilli - finely chopped
1 tsp salt or to taste
¼ tsp red chilli powder or to taste
1 tsp lemon juice
2 tbsp fresh cilantro/coriander leaves - chopped

SALAD TOPPING
1 cup thinly sliced lettuce
1 cup thinly sliced tomato
2 tbsp fresh cilantro/coriander leaves
½ tsp salt
¼ cup grated cheddar cheese
2 tbsp lemon juice

TO SERVE
some home made or ready-made salsa

METHOD

1 To prepare the filling, heat 1 tbsp oil. Add chicken and stir-fry till it changes colour. Cover and let it cook on low heat for 6-7 minutes or till tender.

2 Increase heat and cook till dry and slightly browned. Cool and shred the chicken. Discard bones.

3 Heat 1 tbsp oil in a wok/pan. Add onion and garlic. Cook till soft.

4 Add tomatoes, green chilli, salt and red chilli powder. Cook for 5 minutes or till the tomatoes get soft. Add shredded chicken, lemon juice and fresh cilantro/coriander. Mix well. Cook for 1-2 minutes till dry. Check salt and spices. Keep aside.

5 Mix all the ingredients of the salad together in a bowl and keep aside.

6 Heat taco shells in a preheated oven for a few minutes to warm them.

7 Fill a taco shell partially with hot chicken filling. Top with some salad, then top with some salsa (see p. 9). Repeat with all the shells.

8 Serve immediately with tomato salsa served separately in a bowl.

Spinach Quesadillas

Pronounced 'keseidiayas', since 'll' is pronounced 'y' in Spanish. These quesadillas are made with tortillas that are flavoured with spinach. They are closed over a cheesy corn filling, then pan-fried. A good melting cheese like mozzarella is important for this tasty treat.

Serves 4-6

INGREDIENTS

SPINACH TORTILLAS
2 cups chopped spinach
1½ cups plain flour (*maida*)
½ tsp baking powder, ¼ tsp salt
¼ tsp salt, ¼ cup water, ¼ tsp sugar

FILLING
150 g/5 oz mozzarella cheese - grated
(1½ cups)
50 g/2 oz processed cheddar cheese -
grated (½ cup)
1 green chilli - deseeded and finely
chopped
1 large tomato - chopped without pulp
1 large onion - very finely chopped
½ cup cooked corn
salt and pepper to taste

METHOD

1. To prepare tortillas, puree spinach with ¼ tsp salt, ¼ tsp sugar and ¼ cup water till smooth . Sift flour with baking powder and ¼ tsp salt. Add spinach puree very gradually, adding just enough to get a stiff dough. Knead till smooth and elastic. Make 8 equal balls. Cover with a plastic wrap/cling film or a damp cloth and keep aside for 15 minutes.

2. Roll out each ball using a little flour till you get a very thin round of about 8" diameter.

3. Heat a griddle (*tawa*). Cook lightly on one side for about a minute and then turn. Reduce heat and cook the other side also for a minute till light brown specks appear. Wrap in a thick kitchen towel or aluminium foil and keep aside in a casserole. Make all tortillas in this manner.

4. For the filling, mix both the cheeses together in a bowl. Add a pinch of salt and ½ tsp pepper.

5. In a separate bowl, mix corn, tomato, onion and green chilli. Add ¼ tsp salt and ¼ tsp pepper or to taste.

6. Sprinkle 2 tbsp cheese on half of the tortilla. Leave the other side of the tortilla without any filling.

7. Spread corn mixture on the cheese, on the same side.

8. Sprinkle 2 tbsp cheese again on the corn mixture. Put cheese nicely on the edges.

9. Pick up the side without the filling & fold to make a semicircle. Press well so that the edges stick together.

10. Heat 2 tbsp oil in a pan, fry one quesadilla at a time carefully till crisp golden on both sides. Press the sides to close. Remove to a paper napkin.

11. Cut each into 3 triangular pieces with a pizza cutter. Serve hot with salsa.

Chilli Rellenos (Stuffed Chillies)

Stuffed chillies are popular all over Mexico. The stuffing can be as simple as grated cheese or cottage cheese. Or it can be quite elaborate as given in this delicious recipe.

Gives 7 pieces

INGREDIENTS

7 big pabolano chillies, choose the fat
large green chillies
¼ cup vinegar
½ tsp salt
2-3 tbsp cornstarch

FILLING
1 small potato - chopped (½ cup)
4 tbsp grated carrot
¾ cup boiled (cooked) rice
2 tbsp cheese spread - at room temp.
½ tsp salt
½ tsp ground cumin (*jeera powder*)
½ tsp oregano
½ tsp vinegar

BATTER
½ cup cornstarch
¾ tsp salt
¼ cup water, approx.

METHOD

1. Slit open chillies & remove seeds. Put the chillies in a bowl. Pour vinegar. Sprinkle salt. Rub well. Keep aside for ½ hour.

2. Cut potato into very tiny cubes.

3. Heat oil in a wok and deep-fry potato pieces till golden.

4. For filling, mix fried potato pieces with all the other ingredients given under filling. Mix well.

5. Pick up the chillies and stuff them gently with the filling. Do not break them while stuffing.

6. Grill chillies under a grill till black patches appear on them.

7. Mix all ingredients of the batter in a bowl to get a batter of a thick coating consistency.

8. Roll the chillies over dry cornstarch. Dip one roasted chilli at a time in batter & deep-fry in hot oil to a golden brown colour till crisp. Serve.

main course
dishes

Red Snapper Veracruz-Style

Serves 4

INGREDIENTS

500 g/1 lb red snapper or any other white
fish fillets
2 tbsp olive oil
2 onions - chopped (1 cup)
2 tsp garlic paste
400 g/12 oz tomatoes
10 green olives - pitted and chopped
2 tbsp capers
3 bay leaves (*tej patta*)
¾ tsp peppercorns
1 tsp salt
½ cup cream

METHOD

1 Put whole tomatoes in boiling water. Cover & cook for 3-4 minutes till the skin starts to peel off. Remove from water. Peel and chop finely.

2 Heat oil in a large skillet/pan. Add onion and garlic and fry gently for 5 minutes until soft but not brown. Add tomatoes, olives, capers, bay leaves, peppercorns and salt. Cook for 7-8 minutes.

3 Add fish. Sprinkle a little salt on fish. Mix gently. Add ½ cup water. Bring to a boil, reduce heat, cover and cook for about 7 minutes until fish flakes and breaks off easily when tested with a fork.

4 Add cream, cook for another minute. Check salt. Serve hot.

Chicken Chilli Chimichangas

These tortillas are folded like an envelope over a chicken and mushroom mixture, then deep-fried till crisp. Do try this great Mexican dish – you will surely love it!

Serves 3-4

INGREDIENTS

6 flour tortillas (see p. 7)
250 g/8 oz boneless chicken - cut into ½"
pieces
1½ tsp chopped garlic
¾ tsp red chilli flakes
2 onions - finely chopped
200 g/ 6 oz mushrooms - chopped
1½ tsp oregano, ¾ tsp pepper
1¼ tsp salt
1-2 green chillies - chopped, optional
2 tbsp chopped cilantro/coriander leaves
1 tbsp tomato chilli sauce
1 cup grated cheddar cheese

TO SERVE
some tomato salsa (use ready-made or
see p. 9)
sour cream (use ready-made or see p. 8)

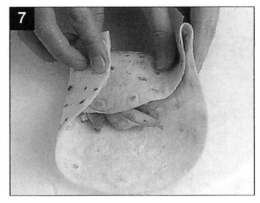

METHOD

1 Make flour tortillas as given on page 7. Keep covered in a thick cloth till required.

2 Heat 2 tbsp oil in a pan. Add chicken and cook on medium heat for 1 minute or till it changes colour. Lower heat and cook covered for 4-5 minutes or till chicken turns tender. Remove chicken from the pan.

3 In the same pan heat 2 tbsp oil or butter. Add garlic and stir-fry for a 30 seconds.

4 Add red chilli flakes. Wait for few seconds.

5 Add chopped onion and mushrooms. Stir fry for 3-4 minutes.

6 Add oregano, green chillies, pepper, salt, cooked chicken, fresh cilantro/coriander leaves and tomato chilli sauce. Mix well and remove from heat.

7 Place one tortilla on a plate. Put 3 tbsp of filling in the centre and add 1-2 tbsp grated cheese over it. Fold one side over the filling, holding on, turn the left and right side a little, to enclose the filling. Fold over again to make a parcel. Repeat with all the tortillas.

8 Heat some oil in a skillet/pan. Fry the chimichangas with the joint side down. Turn over and fry till golden brown. Serve hot with tomato salsa and sour cream.

Note: *If tortillas have been made earlier warm them slightly so that they can be easily folded.*

Tex Mex Beans with Dumplings

Serves 4

INGREDIENTS

DUMPLINGS
3 tbsp cornmeal (*makai ka atta*)
4 tbsp flour (*maida*)
½ tsp salt
1¾ tsp baking powder
2 egg whites
a little milk (3-4 tbsp)

TEX MEX BEANS
4 tbsp oil
1½ tsp chopped garlic
2 medium onions - finely chopped (1 cup)
4 green chillies - chopped finely
1 green bell pepper - chopped finely
1½ tsp salt
1 tsp red chilli powder or to taste
6 tbsp tomato sauce
1 tin of baked beans (450 g/1 lb)

METHOD

1. Mix all the ingredients for the dumplings in a small bowl. Add enough milk to get a dropping consistency. Keep aside.

2. For tex mex beans, heat 4 tbsp oil in a wide frying pan. Add garlic and onion and cook till soft.

3. Add green chillies and green bell pepper. Fry for 1-2 minutes.

4. Add salt, red chilli powder, tomato sauce, baked beans and 2½ cups water. Mix well. Give 1 boil.

5. When the mixture starts boiling add the dumpling batter to the pan, 1 tsp at a time, to get about 12-13 dumplings. Cover with a lid. Boil on medium heat undisturbed for 8-10 minutes or till dumplings get cooked. Serve with grilled bread.

Chicken Burritos with Sauce

These burritos, made with tortillas and filled with a rice add chicken filling, are pan-fried to give them a unique twist. A tasty red sauce is poured over them.

Serves 3-4

INGREDIENTS

6 flour tortillas (see p. 7)

RED SAUCE
2 dry, red chillies
500 g/1 lb tomatoes
1½ tsp crushed garlic
¾ tsp salt
¾ cup ready-made chicken stock
¾ tsp dried basil or thyme (optional)
¾ tsp dried oregano
3½ tbsp tomato sauce
a big pinch of orange red colour (optional)

FILLING
400 g/12 oz boneless chicken - cut into
½" pieces
1½ cups boiled (cooked) rice
4 tbsp butter, 2 tbsp oil
2 tsp chopped garlic
2 tbsp flour (*maida*)
1½ cups milk, ½ tsp salt
6 tbsp grated cheddar cheese
2 tbsp chopped pickled jalapenos
6 tbsp chopped fresh cilantro/coriander

METHOD

1 Make tortillas as given on page 7. Keep aside.

2 Roast the chillies and tomatoes under a grill till black patches appear on them. Do not peel the tomatoes, chop with the peel. If you like, deseed the chillies. Break chillies into small pieces.

3 Place the roasted chillies, tomatoes and all other ingredients for the red sauce in a mixer. Blend well to a fine puree.

4 Heat 1 tbsp oil in a pan. Add the prepared sauce, give one boil. Cook for 3-4 minutes till it becomes slightly thick. Remove from heat, keep sauce aside.

5 For the filling, heat 4 tbsp butter and 1 tbsp oil. Add garlic. Stir fry for 30 seconds.

6 Add chicken and cook till the pieces get lightly browned from all sides. Cook covered on low heat for 5 minutes or till tender.

7 Reduce heat. Add 3 tbsp cheese. Add flour. Mix & stir fry for 1 minute.

8 Add milk and cook stirring till the sauce just starts to get thick. Remove from heat.

9 Add boiled rice, chopped jalapenos & cilantro/coriander. Mix gently so that the rice grains do not break. Check for salt.

10 To assemble, place 3-4 tbsp of filling on a tortilla, a little away from one end. Fold over and roll forward to get a roll. Repeat with the remaining filling and tortillas.

11 To serve, warm the rolls in a microwave or saute in just 1-2 tbsp oil in a pan, with the tucked side down first in oil. Turn, using 2 spoons & cook till light golden from all the sides.

12 Heat the sauce. Pour some hot sauce on the burritos and serve garnished with the remaining 3 tbsp cheese.

Fajitas

Arrange all the ingredients separately on the table – tortillas, hot vegetable filling, salad, sour cream and tomato salsa. Assemble a tortilla with these ingredients and enjoy a freshly rolled delicious wrap!

Makes 5-6

INGREDIENTS

6 flour tortillas (see p. 7)

VEGETABLE FILLING
1 cup small florets of cauliflower
1½ cups shredded cabbage
½ cup French beans - sliced diagonally
2 carrots - sliced diagonally
3 tbsp olive oil, 1 tbsp butter
1 onion - sliced
6 flakes garlic - crushed
2 dry, red chillies - crushed
½ tsp freshly ground peppercorns
1 tsp salt
1 tsp vinegar
2 tbsp chopped cilantro/coriander
2 tsp white wine (optional)
5-6 fingers of fresh mozzarella or *paneer*

SALAD
3-4 lettuce leaves - shredded
1-2 green onions - chopped with the greens
½ tsp salt, 1 tomato - chopped
1 green chilli - chopped
½ cup cheddar cheese - grated

ACCOMPANIMENTS
sour cream (see p. 8)
tomato salsa (see p. 9)

METHOD

1. Make tortillas as given on page 7. Keep covered in a thick cloth till required.

2. For the salad, mix all ingredients of the salad in a bowl. Mix well.

3. For the filling, heat 3 tbsp oil and 1 tbsp butter. Cook onions and garlic till soft. Add all the four vegetables. Stir well to mix. Add red chillies, pepper, 1 tsp salt and vinegar. Stir-fry for 5-7 minutes on moderate heat till tender but still crisp. Add coriander and wine. Cook for 2-3 minutes. Add mozzarella or *paneer* fingers. Remove from heat. Mix well.

4. To serve, put sour cream, salad and salsa in separate bowls. Put warm tortillas wrapped in a napkin in a casserole. Serve hot vegetable filling separately in a sizzler plate.

5. Make your own fajita - take one tortilla, spread 1-2 tsp of the sour cream on the whole tortilla spreading till the sides. Put some vegetables on it, then sprinkle some salad. Finally dot with 1½ tbsp salsa. Roll up and enjoy!

Shrimps/Prawns in Pumpkin Seed Sauce

Serves 4-5

INGREDIENTS

300 g/10 oz medium-sized shrimps
(cleaned and deveined)
3 tbsp pumpkin seeds
or
melon seeds (*magaz*)
2 tbsp oil/butter
1 tsp chopped garlic
1 medium onion - chopped (½ cup)
2 jalapenos or green chillies - chopped
4 tomatoes - pureed in a mixer
1½ tsp ground coriander (*dhania powder*)
1 tsp ground cumin (*jeera powder*)
1 tsp sugar
1¼ tsp salt (will depend on the saltiness
of shrimps/prawns)
½ cup water
2 tsp cornstarch dissolved in ¼ cup of
water
3 tsp chopped parsley

METHOD

1 On a griddle or pan, toast the pumpkin seeds on medium heat and coarsely grind them. Keep aside.

2 Heat oil or butter in a pan. Add garlic. Fry for 1 minute.

3 Add onion and cook till soft.

4 Add jalapeno/green chillies and the prepared tomato puree. Add ground coriander, ground cumin, sugar and salt. Give one boil.

5 Add shrimps/prawns. Mix well. Cover and lower heat. Cook for about 4-5 minutes till the shrimps/prawns are tender. Add water and cook for 2 minutes.

6 When shrimps/prawns are tender add pumpkin seeds. Cook for a minute till sauce is slightly thick. Remove from heat.

7 Serve hot with rice, garnished with fresh parsley sprigs.

Veggie Enchiladas

Makes 6 Enchiladas

INGREDIENTS

6 corn or flour tortillas (see. p. 8 or p. 7)

FILLING
¾ cup ready-made baked beans
1 cup crumbled feta cheese or cottage cheese (*paneer*)
1 tbsp oil, 1 tsp chopped garlic
1-2 green onions - chop finely along with the green part (½ cup)
½ green bell pepper - chopped finely (½ cup)
½ tsp salt, or to taste
1 tsp oregano, ½ tsp red chilli flakes

SAUCE
¾ tsp chopped garlic
½ cup ready-made tomato puree
3 medium tomatoes - pureed in the mixer
1 tsp sugar, ½ tsp salt or to taste
1 tsp red chilli flakes
1 tsp oregano
½-¾ cup grated mozzarella cheese

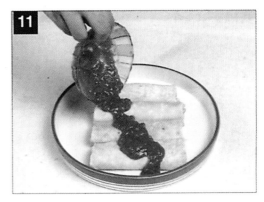

METHOD

1. Make corn or flour tortillas as given on page 8 or 7. Keep aside covered in a thick cloth till required.

2. For the filling, heat 1 tbsp oil. Add garlic and green onions. Stir till soft. Add green bell pepper. Stir.

3. Add salt, oregano, red chilli flakes, baked beans and crumbled cheese. Cook till dry. Remove from heat.

4. For the sauce, heat 1 tbsp oil. Add garlic. Stir.

5. Add all other ingredients of the sauce. Cook for 4-5 minutes on low heat till sauce thickens. Remove from heat. The sauce should not be runny.

6. Heat 1 tsp oil in a pan. Fry the prepared tortillas one at a time in hot oil on both sides for few seconds. Do not let the tortillas turn crisp and brown. Repeat to fry the remaining tortillas in the same way. Keep them wrapped in a cloth in a box, till required.

7. To assemble, take a tortilla, keep it on a flat surface, spread 1 tbsp of sauce on it covering the tortilla completely.

8. Place some filling in a line in the center of the tortilla and roll forward to make an enchilada (see p. 6). Repeat with all the remaining tortillas.

9. Take an oven proof serving plate or dish, place the rolled enchiladas with the tucked side down in a row in the baking dish.

10. Pour the rest of the sauce on the enchiladas, sprinkle with grated cheese. Cover dish with aluminium foil and bake in a preheated oven at 200°C/400°F for 20 minutes. Serve hot.

Meat Mince & Bean Pie

Serves 4

INGREDIENTS

BASE OR SHELL
1/3 cup melted butter
1½ cups plain flour (*maida*)
3 tbsp water or as required
¼ cup grated cheddar cheese

FILLING
250 g/8 oz ground meat or mince (*keema*)
1 cup boiled red kidney beans (*rajmah*)
2 tsp vinegar
3 tbsp oil, 1 onion - finely chopped
1 tbsp chopped garlic
1 tsp salt
1 tsp red chilli powder or to taste
2 tomatoes - finely chopped
2 tbsp chopped fresh cilantro/coriander leaves
¾-1 cup grated cheddar cheese

METHOD

1 To prepare the base, combine the butter and flour, rubbing well until it looks like breadcrumbs. Add cheese to the mixture. Add just enough water to bind and gather lightly to a firm dough. Keep aside covered in a damp cloth for 20 minutes.

2 Roll out to a big round chappati and place in a buttered 9 inch loose bottom pie or flan tin. Press carefully to get a well levelled base, covering the whole of the bottom and the sides also. Remove extra dough from the sides by pressing dough on the edges to cut so that you get a neat shell. Prick with a fork all over to avoid the crust from puffing up during baking. Bake the

pie shell in a hot oven at 200°C/400°F, for about 15 minutes, until light golden. Allow to cool.

3 For the filling, heat 3 tbsp oil in a pan. Add onion and garlic and cook till onion turns soft.

4 Add meat mince and stir for 5 minutes, stirring continuously.

5 Add salt, red chilli powder and chopped tomatoes, stir fry for 3-4 minutes.

6 Add 1 cup water. Mix well. Boil for 7-8 minutes on high heat. Keep on low heat for another 5 minutes. Remove from heat when tender.

7 Add beans and vinegar to mince and return to heat.

8 Cook till almost dry but not completely dry. Add fresh cilantro/coriander. Mix well.

9 Place the filling in the pie shell. Sprinkle cheese.

10 To serve, heat the pie in the oven for 5-7 minutes till cheese melts. Serve hot.

Bean & Corn Burritos

Makes 4-5

INGREDIENTS

4- 5 corn tortillas (see p. 8)

FILLING
1 cup tinned corn
1 cup baked beans in tomato sauce (½ tin)
1 green bell pepper - chopped (1 cup)
2 tbsp pickled jalapenos - chopped
1 cup grated cheddar cheese
4 tbsp oil
2 tsp garlic - chopped finely
1 medium onion - finely chopped
½ tsp red chilli flakes or powder
½ tsp ground cumin (*jeera powder*)
½ tsp ground coriander (*dhania powder*)
½ tsp salt, or to taste
2- 3 drops of tabasco sauce

TOPPING
some tomato salsa (see p. 9)
some sour cream (see p. 8)

METHOD

1 Make tortillas as given on page 8. Keep covered in a thick cloth.

2 For the filling, heat oil. Add garlic and onion. Cook till onion turns soft.

3 Add corn and chopped green bell pepper. Add tabasco. Cook for 3-4 minutes.

4 Add jalapenos, grated cheese and all the seasonings. Mix well.

5 Add baked beans. Mix well. Remove from heat. Keep aside.

6 Warm a tortilla slightly on a hot griddle or you can also fry them with a little oil. Do not make them crisp as then they will not fold well.

7 Put some bean and corn mixture down the centre of the tortilla and sprinkle some cheese on it. Roll up the tortilla like a burrito (see p. 6).

8 Wrap the burritos in paper or cloth towels and microwave on 50% to warm them. Alternately, heat 5 tbsp oil in a pan, place the burritos, tucked side down and shallow-fry till light golden. Turn, using 2 flat spoons and cook till golden brown on both sides.

9 Top with some tomato salsa & sour cream and serve immediately.

rice

White Pilaf with Cheese

Serves 4

INGREDIENTS

1 cup long-grained rice - washed and kept in the strainer for 20 minutes
3 tbsp butter or oil
1 medium onion - finely chopped
1 cup tinned corn niblets
4-5 green chillies - finely chopped (adjust to taste)
4 tbsp chopped fresh cilantro/coriander leaves
1½ tsp salt
¾ cup crumbled feta cheese or paneer

METHOD

1 Wash rice and keep in a strainer to drain water for 20 minutes. Do not soak.

2 Heat oil or butter in a heavy-based deep pan. Add onion and stir fry till onion turns soft.

3 Add corn, rice, 2 green chillies and fresh cilantro/coriander. Stir gently for 2-3 minutes till the rice gets toasted.

4 Add salt and 2 cups water. Give one boil. Reduce heat and cook covered for 10 minutes on very low heat.

5 When just a little water remains, add crumbled feta cheese. Mix gently with a fork. Cover and cook on low heat for another 5 minutes or till all the water is absorbed and rice is soft.

6 Fluff with a fork and serve hot garnished with fresh cilantro/coriander and green chillies.

Spicy Shrimp Pilaf

Serves 4

INGREDIENTS

1 cup long-grained rice - washed and kept
in the strainer for 20 minutes
250 g/8 oz small shrimps/prawns
6 tbsp oil/butter
1¼ tsp salt
½-1 tsp red chilli powder

PASTE

4 whole, dry, red chillies - soaked in water
for 15-20 minutes and drained
1 large flake garlic
1 medium onion
1 medium tomato

METHOD

1 Wash rice and leave in a strainer to drain water for 20 minutes.

2 Devein and wash shrimps/prawns well.

3 Soak whole red chillies in water for 15-20 minutes.

4 Grind together soaked red chillies, onion, tomato and garlic. Use little water if required.

5 Heat 3 tbsp oil/butter in a skillet. Add ground paste. Fry well till nearly dry.

6 Add shrimps/prawns. Fry for only 2-3 minutes till shrimps/prawns change colour. Keep aside.

7 In another deep pan heat 3 tbsp oil/butter. Add rice and fry till rice starts to brown. (It acquires a light brown toasted colour).

8 Add prawn mixture, salt, red chilli powder and mix well.

9 Add 2 cups of water. Cover and give one boil.

10 Lower heat and let it cook for 12-15 minutes or till rice is tender and all the water is absorbed.

11 Fluff with a fork and serve garnished with lemon wedges and fresh cilantro/coriander sprigs.

Note: *Replace shrimps/prawns, with chicken or vegetables or a combination of all three to make variations of pilaf according to this method.*

desserts

Rice Pudding

Rice is a popular dessert ingredient in Mexico. This is a light, easy to make rice pudding, which is full of flavour.

Serves 6-8

INGREDIENTS

½ cup rice
2 cups milk, 1 cup water
2" cinnamon stick (*dalchini*)
¼ cup sugar
rind of 1 lemon (peel thinly, only the outer yellow skin)
2 eggs
½ cup raisins (*kishmish*)
1½ tbsp rum, 1 tbsp butter
1-2 pinches of cinnamon powder - to sprinkle

METHOD

1 Put rice, lemon rind and water in a saucepan and bring to a boil.

Cover and cook for 10 minutes on low heat. Remove lemon peel.

2 Add sugar, milk and cinnamon stick. Stir well for 2 minutes.

3 Remove from heat. Let it cool slightly. Mix in egg yolks.

4 Beat egg whites till stiff. Add beaten egg whites to the rice-milk mixture and fold gently.

5 Add raisins. Transfer to a baking dish and bake for 15 minutes at 180°C/350°F till very light golden.

6 Sprinkle cinnamon powder. Serve hot or at room temperature or chilled.

GLOSSARY OF NAMES/TERMS

Avocado	A green fruit which turns blackish as it ripens. Used for the popular Mexican relish - "Guacamole"
Appetizers	Small tasty bits of food served before meals.
Aubergine	Brinjal/eggplant
Bake	To cook by dry heat usually in an oven or a tandoor.
Batter	Any mixture of flour and liquid which is beaten or stirred to make a pouring consistency.
Beans	Dried black beans and red kidney beans are most popular in Mexico
Blanch	To remove skin by dipping into hot water for a couple of minutes. e.g. to blanch tomatoes or almonds.
Blend	To combine two or more ingredients.
Capers	Buds of a flowering plant. They are usually available pickled in bottles.
Capsicums	Bell peppers
Chappati	The Indian unleavened flat bread which resembles tortillas in looks and taste.
Caramelize	To heat sugar till it turns brown.
Consistency	A term describing the texture, usually the thickness of a mixture.
Coriander	Cilantro
Corn meal	White or yellow flour prepared from corn.
Cornstarch	Cornflour
Cream	In sauces, light cream or half and half will do, in desserts use whipping or heavy cream
Dot	To put small amounts of butter.
Dice	To cut into small neat cubes.
Dough	A mixture of flour, liquid etc., kneaded together into a stiff paste or roll.
Drain	To remove liquid from food.
Garnish	To decorate.
Jalapeno	A kind of green pepper which is not too hot.
Marinate	To soak food in a mixture for some time so that the flavour of the mixture penetrates into the food.
Paneer	Indian cheese made by curdling milk, resembles tofu.
Plain flour	All purpose flour, maida
Puree	A smooth mixture obtained by rubbing cooked vegetables or blanched tomatoes through a sieve.
Saute	To toss and make light brown in shallow fat.
Spring onions	Green onions, scallions.
Stock	Broth or you may mix seasoning cubes in water to get stock
Toss	To lightly mix ingredients without mashing them e.g. for salads.
Whip	To incorporate air by beating and thus increase the volume as in egg whites and whipped cream.